GEOLOGY

A SCIENCE ACTIVITY BOOK

BY

PAT AND BARBARA WARD

COPYRIGHT ©1994 Mark Twain Media, Inc.

ISBN   10-digit: 1-58037-042-X
        13-digit: 978-1-58037-042-4

Printing No. CD-1807

Mark Twain Media, Inc., Publishers
Distributed by Carson-Dellosa Publishing Company, Inc.

TABLE OF CONTENTS

Earth
An Introduction

"Ladies and gentlemen, please make yourselves comfortable and fasten your safety straps. We are about to begin our journey.

"We are about to leave the far reaches of the universe. We will move rapidly among the millions of galaxies as we head toward the cluster known as the Local Group. Once we enter the Local Group we will be looking for a medium-sized spiral galaxy called the Milky Way. About two thirds of the way from the center of the galaxy, along one of the arms, we will locate an average-sized yellow star. This star is the center of a solar system consisting of nine planets and their satellites, an asteroid belt, and assorted comets and meteoroids. Our final destination is the third planet from the sun, the one called Earth.

"As you look out of our spacecraft, you will notice that Earth is a beautiful, spherical planet. The largest percentage of the planet is blue oceans and waterways. There are also large areas of lush, green vegetation and sections of brown deserts. Closely surrounding the planet is a continuously changing layer of white clouds. It is a marvelous sight. The true wonder of this planet, however, is in the fact that it sustains life, from tiny single-celled organisms to large mammals—a great variety in all.

"As we reflect on the meaning of this—one of the true marvels of the universe—we must realize that the location of this planet may be largely responsible for its beauty. If Earth were closer to its parent sun, the climate would be too hot to sustain the lush vegetation. The large blue oceans and waterways would probably evaporate. There would be tremendous doses of radiation attacking the planet, and life would not be able to exist under these conditions. On the other hand, if Earth were any farther from its sun, the temperatures would be too cold. Again, the lush vegetation would not survive, and the blue waters would become solid blocks of ice. There would not be enough light to sustain life.

"Thank you for your kind attention during this trip. We have now completed our journey and are making final preparations for our landing. Please make sure all luggage is safely stored in the overhead compartments or beneath the seat in front of you. Please check that all seats and trays are in their upright and locked positions. Thank you all for traveling with us. We hope your stay on Earth is a good one and that you will travel with us again soon."

The Solar System

Name _____   Date _____

For the student:

1. In what type of galaxy do we live?

_____

_____

_____

2. What size is our sun?

_____

_____

_____

3. How would Earth be different if it were closer to the sun?

_____

_____

_____

4. How would Earth be different if it were farther from the sun?

_____

_____

_____

5. There are actual pictures of Earth taken from space. How was that possible?

_____

_____

_____

The Formation of Earth

Scientists believe that a great cloud of dust and gas floating in space began to collapse on itself approximately 4.6 billion years ago. Matter from the central portion of the cloud formed a sun, which is now the center of our solar system. The remaining matter formed a disk surrounding the sun.

During the following 100 million years or so, small particles in the disk of matter collided with each other and formed larger units of matter. Eventually they were large enough to be labeled as *planetesimals.*

The planetesimals continued to collide and combine until small planets were formed. The infant planet Earth came into being.

The heat of the continued collisions with planetoids kept the young, small planet in a molten state. As matter continued to be added, heavy metals, such as iron and nickel, sank to the center of the planet, forming a core.

Meanwhile, solar winds slowly cleared the surrounding space of many of the tiny particles of matter. As the space cleared, there were fewer and fewer collisions. The planet began to cool. As the planet cooled, its layers began to separate. The top layer cooled the most, forming a crust surrounding the planet.

Picture the Formation

Below are five drawings that illustrate the way the Earth may have formed. Write a good paragraph explaining each of the diagrams. Be sure you remember all those rules you have learned about proper grammar, punctuation, etc.!

The Structure of Earth

If you were asked to describe, in detail, the setup of your classroom, you should be able to do that. You would look around you and carefully note the shape of the room, placement of doors and windows, and the number of bulletin boards and chalkboards. You would describe the number of desks and chairs and how they were arranged. You could add many details about the materials that you are so familiar with and use so often.

The reason that you could successfully and accurately complete this task is that you can use *direct observation.* You can see and feel the objects and their locations. Direct observations can make this kind of task much easier to perform!

Scientists have described the internal, or inside, structure of the Earth. The problem that the scientists have been faced with is that they cannot make direct observations. They must gather lots of information, analyze the data, and then develop theories. Scientists are always looking for more information. As they collect new data and analyze it, scientists may decide to change their ideas or theories. It is a process that never seems to end.

How can scientists collect information about something they cannot see or observe directly? One method they can use involves drilling into the Earth. They can bring out sections from holes as deep as 8 kilometers (5 miles) into the Earth. The problem with this method is that the Earth is about 6,370 kilometers (3,958 miles) deep! Another way that scientists have collected data is by using seismographic equipment. These tools measure the *seismic,* or shock, waves produced by earthquakes. Analyzing this data has given scientists valuable insight into the structure of our planet.

Once the information is collected and the data is analyzed, the theories are developed. From these theories, scientists are able to create *models.* Just as the theories may change when new information is learned, the models may change as well.

Currently, scientists believe the Earth is made of four layers: the crust, the mantle, the outer core, and the inner core. Using this model, scientists have been able to explain many geological events such as earthquakes, volcanoes, the movement of continents, etc. With this model, scientists hope to develop a better understanding of the past of our planet so they might better understand the current events and better predict the future of our home.

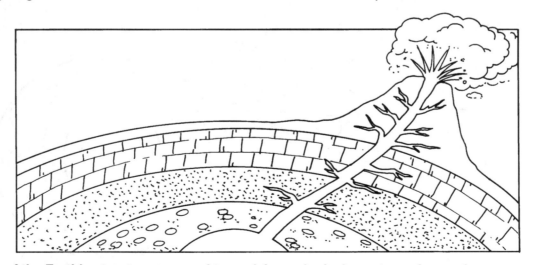

Models of the Earth's structure are used to explain geological events such as volcanoes.

Name _____   Date _____

For the student:

1. Do scientists know how the planet Earth was formed? Why or why not? _____

_____

2. How do scientists develop their ideas or theories about the formation of the stars and planets?

_____

_____

3. Why is it important to know about the beginning of the planet? _____

_____

4. Why would the heavier metals sink to the center during the formation of a planet?

_____

_____

5. What is the outermost layer of the Earth called?_____

6. What is direct observation? _____

_____

7. Why is it difficult for scientists to know what the inside of the Earth is like? _____

_____

8. How can they learn anything about the inside of the Earth? _____

_____

9. What is a model? _____

_____

10. According to the current model of the Earth, what are the Earth's layers?_____

_____

The Earth's Crust

Think of an egg and its parts. The yolk is in the center, then there is the white of the egg, and it is all surrounded by a thin shell. The Earth can be compared to an egg. It also has three parts: the *core* is in the center, then there is the *mantle,* and it is all surrounded by the *crust.*

As far as scientists know now, all life exists either on the surface or within the first few meters of the crust.

The crust is made up of different kinds of rocks. The upper crust is made primarily of *sedimentary* rocks. These rocks are formed when materials on the Earth's surface are worn away. They are then deposited in layers that form several different kinds of sedimentary rock. Underneath these layers, the crust is made of igneous and metamorphic rocks. *Igneous* rocks form when magma, or molten rock, cools either deep within the Earth or near its surface. *Metamorphic* rocks are formed when sedimentary or igneous rocks are changed due to extreme heat and pressure. The igneous and metamorphic rocks form a solid layer of the crust, which is known as *bedrock.*

There are approximately 90 different chemical substances, or elements, that have been identified in the Earth's crust. Five of them, however, make up more than 90 percent of the crust: oxygen, silicon, aluminum, iron, and calcium. Sodium, potassium, and magnesium are among the most commonly found elements in the remaining ten percent of the crust.

The elements and compounds found within the crust provide many of the energy resources we depend on for survival and comfort, including gas, coal, and oil. They also provide the metals we commonly use, such as gold, iron, and lead. Minerals that have found important places in our lives are also provided by the Earth's crust: diamonds, quartz, and graphite.

Scientists refer to the crust as the *lithosphere,* the solid portion of the Earth. The word *litho* comes from the Greek word meaning rock or stone. The scientists believe that Earth's crust, or lithosphere, is broken into several segments or *plates.* They also believe that these crustal plates move, or drift, on hot molten material that is beneath the crust.

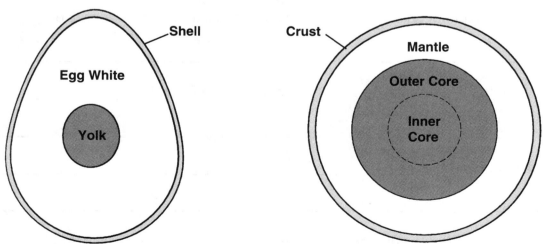

The layers of the Earth can be compared to those of an egg.

Thin Crust or Thick Crust?

The thin, outer layer of the Earth's surface can be divided into two kinds of crust: continental crust and ocean crust.

As you might expect, continental crust is found under the landforms or continents. This crust is usually about 35 kilometers (22 miles) thick; however, it may be up to 70 kilometers (43 miles) thick in mountainous areas.

This type of crust may be subdivided into two layers. The first layer is called the *sial.* It is made of granite-like rock. Granite is a light-colored igneous rock.

The second layer of crust is called the *sima,* and it is made of basalt-like rock. Basalt is a dark-colored igneous rock that is denser than granite.

The sima layer of the continental crust extends beyond the edges of the continents, under the oceans, and forms the oceanic crust. This is a much thinner kind of crust, averaging only 5–7 kilometers (3–4 miles) in thickness. Scientists estimate that the very top layer, up to half a mile thick, is sediment that has washed into the oceans as the continental crust has eroded. The ocean crust is relatively young, and new crust is being formed continuously as active volcanoes erupt along the ocean floor.

Look at the diagram below. Carefully label the general structures of the Earth's crust: sima layer, mountain, ocean, sial layer.

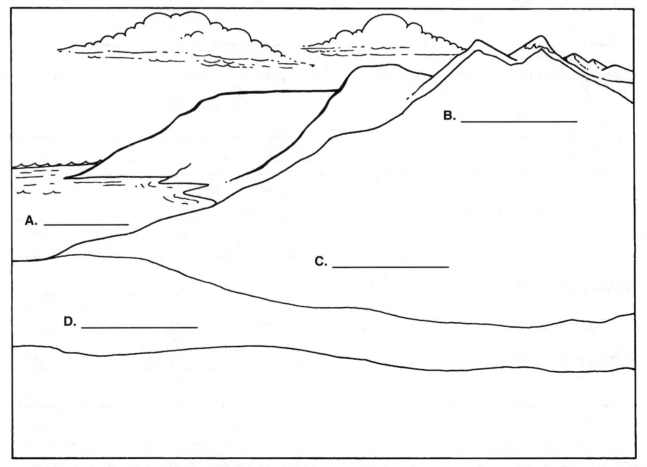

Name _____   Date _____

For the student:

1. How are each of the following kinds of rock formed?

     sedimentary _____

     igneous _____

     metamorphic _____

2. What is the bedrock layer? _____

_____

3. What are the five most abundant elements in the Earth's crust? _____

_____

4. What is the lithosphere? _____

_____

5. What do scientists believe is happening to the segments of Earth's crust, which are called *plates?*

_____

_____

6. What is the ocean crust? _____

_____

7. What are the two layers of continental crust called? _____

8. Which layer continues under the oceans to form the ocean crust?_____

9. Why is the sima layer found beneath the sial layer? _____

_____

_____

Name _____   Date _____

Elements in the Crust

The chart below shows eight of the most commonly found elements in the Earth's crust. Refer to a Periodic Table of the Elements to find the symbol for each element. Add the correct symbols to the chart. Then, using the information provided in the table, answer the questions below.

Element	Symbol	Weight %	Atomic %	Volume %
Oxygen	_____	46.6	62.6	93.8
Silicon	_____	27.7	21.2	0.9
Aluminum	_____	8.1	6.5	0.5
Iron	_____	5.0	1.9	1.4
Calcium	_____	3.6	1.9	1.0
Sodium	_____	2.8	2.6	1.3
Potassium	_____	2.6	1.4	1.8
Magnesium	_____	2.1	1.8	0.3

1. What is the most commonly found element in the Earth's crust? _____

2. Which two elements make up more than 80 percent of the atoms found in the Earth's crust?

_____

3. Oxygen makes up more than 90 percent of the volume of the Earth's crust. Is oxygen found as a solid, liquid, or gas?

_____

4. Why do you think a gas would take up more volume than any of the solids?

_____

5. Which element would be most abundant, by weight, in the minerals and rocks that are in the crust? Why did you pick that element?

_____

The Mantle

Let's think about an egg and its parts again. Remember, we compared the shell of an egg to the crust of the Earth. Just inside the shell is a thin membrane and the white of the egg. Let's see how that compares to the Earth's mantle.

Just below the Earth's crust is an area known as the *Mohorovicic Discontinuity,* or the *Moho.* In 1909, a Yugoslavian scientist named Adrija Mohorovicic, using data collected from seismographic studies, discovered a boundary separating the crust from the mantle. This area has been recognized as a distinct break between the two layers.

Below the Moho lies the Earth's mantle. This layer is believed to be about 2,900 kilometers (1,800 miles) thick. It makes up 80 percent of the Earth's total volume and 68 percent of its mass. This is the heaviest part of the Earth.

The mantle appears to be composed of silicon, oxygen, aluminum, iron, and magnesium. There seem to be greater percentages of iron deeper into the mantle.

Geologists believe that the mantle is solid rock, which is denser rock than that of the crust above it. The density of the mantle itself seems to increase as the depth increases. This may be due to the increased amount of iron deeper into the mantle.

Scientists have developed a model of the mantle that designates the first 100 kilometers (62 miles) as very rigid rock. From that point to a depth of 250 kilometers (155 miles), they believe the mantle is close to its melting point. The rock has reached a point of plasticity, but it has not changed from a solid form to a true liquid. It does not actually melt, due to the great pressure exerted upon it by the materials above. From the 250-kilometer line to the edge of the mantle at 2,900 kilometers, it is assumed to be rigid, solid matter again.

The plastic-like rock material in the 100- to 250-kilometer zone seems to flow, almost like syrup. This is magma, which is moving by the weight of the landmasses and oceans pressing down upon it.

The amount of pressure in the mantle increases as the depth of the mantle increases. Temperatures follow a similar pattern. Scientists believe temperatures may vary from 870 degrees Celsius (1,600 degrees Fahrenheit) at the top edge of the mantle to 2,200 degrees Celsius (4,000 degrees Fahrenheit) near the core.

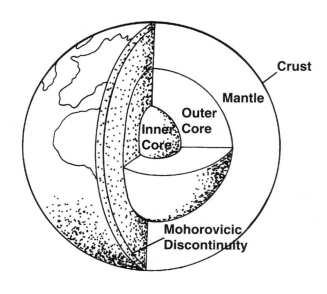

Earth
Student Research

Divide the class into small groups to complete the following research project.

People are naturally curious, and they are constantly striving to learn more about the unknown. One of the great mysteries for scientists is the exact structure of the Earth. They have been able to drill into the Earth's crust, but not beyond. Two projects were recently designed to seek answers to some of the questions that have been puzzling scientists for years.

Using resource materials, research one of the following projects:

  • Project Mohole, begun March 1961

  • Deep-Sea Drilling Project, begun 1968

Be sure you answer the following questions while you are doing your research:

1. What were the goals of the project?

2. Where did the project take place?

3. How long did the project last?

4. What were the results of the project?

When you have finished gathering all your information, organize your answers so they may be displayed in a poster format. Ask your teacher for details as to the finished size, etc.

The Core

The final section of the Earth might be compared to the yolk of an egg, just as the mantle was similar to the white, and the crust resembled the shell. With the current theory of the Earth's structure, however, scientists believe the core is really two layers: an outer core and an inner core. Let's compare the two.

The Outer Core

This section of the Earth is believed to be 2,250 kilometers (1,398 miles) deep.

Temperatures range from 2,200 degrees Celsius (3,992 degrees Fahrenheit) to 5,000 degrees Celsius (9,032 degrees Fahrenheit) as you descend farther into this section of core.

Scientists believe the outer core is liquid and consists of very dense, melted iron and nickel.

The core's dense iron is believed to create an effect similar to the magnetic field that surrounds a magnet. This is how scientists explain the presence of Earth's magnetic field.

The Inner Core

This section of the Earth is believed to be 1,300 kilometers (808 miles) deep from its edge to the center of the Earth.

Temperatures are believed to be approximately 5,000 degrees Celsius (9,032 degrees Fahrenheit) throughout this section.

Scientists believe the inner core is solid and consists of very dense, solid iron and nickel.

The inner core remains solid due to the immense pressure exerted on it. The pressure may be 2 million times stronger than normal pressure exerted on Earth's surface.

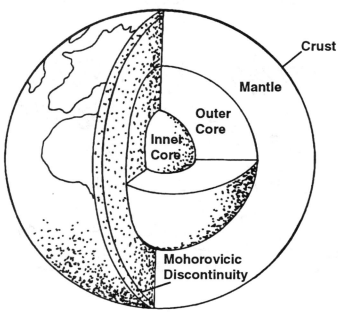

Name _____   Date _____

For the student:

1. Which part of an egg compares to the Moho? _____

2. Which part of an egg compares to the mantle? _____

3. What do scientists believe explains the increased density of material deeper into the mantle?

_____

_____

4. What happens to temperatures in the mantle? _____

_____

5. Why does part of the mantle appear to flow? _____

_____

6. How deep is the total core of the Earth? _____

7. What is the main difference between the inner core and the outer core? _____

_____

8. Why does that difference exist? _____

_____

9. How do scientists explain the presence of a magnetic field around the Earth? _____

_____

10. Why is there so much more pressure exerted on the Earth's core than on the Earth's surface?

_____

_____

How Do You Find the Core?

Geologists have been able to drill down into the crust. The rocks they have extracted have given them lots of clues about the formation and structure of the Earth. They have tried to drill into the mantle, as well. It would be impossible for them to drill through the crust and the mantle into the core using modern technology. So, how do scientists have any idea what the center of the Earth is like?

Geologists have studied *seismic waves,* or shock waves, that are created by earthquake activity. They have been able to identify different types of waves and have observed their behavior.

Two kinds of seismic waves are S-waves and P-waves. One difference between the waves is their behavior in liquids. P-waves move very slowly in liquids, compared to their speed traveling through solids. S-waves disappear completely when they encounter liquids.

Scientists have collected information that indicates that S-waves and P-waves behave very differently at a depth of 2,900 kilometers (1,800 miles), the beginning of the Earth's outer core. The P-waves slow down and the S-waves disappear. Scientists have also learned that P-waves increase their speed again beginning at a depth of 5,150 kilometers (3,200 miles). This is where scientists believe the inner core begins.

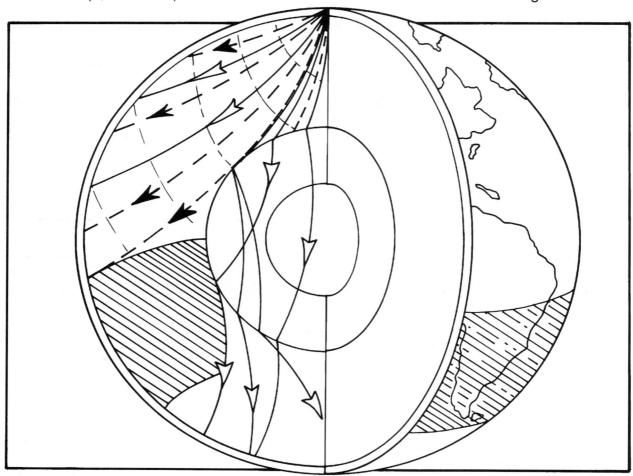

The S-waves, indicated by solid arrows, do not travel through the liquid of the outer core. The white arrows show the paths of P-waves as they travel through the core.

Some Like It Hot

Why is the center of the Earth so hot? Scientists calculate the temperature at the center of the Earth to be approximately 5,000 degrees Celsius (9,032 degrees Fahrenheit), but they are not sure exactly why it is so hot. Here are three theories that might explain the phenomenon:

THEORY #1

When the Earth was formed, the entire planet was hot. Some of this heat may have been created by the continual collisions of planetoids into the young planet as it was forming. After the collisions subsided, the surface of the planet was able to cool, while the interior remained hot. It might be compared to an apple pie that has just come out of the oven. The surface of the pie will eventually cool, but the filling will remain hot.

THEORY #2

A second theory suggests that the great pressure exerted on material deep within the Earth is responsible for creating the high temperatures. The pressure may be as great as several thousand kilograms of pressure per centimeter.

THEORY #3

A third idea is that there are radioactive materials deep within the Earth. As these materials age, they begin to decompose. During this process of aging and decomposing, heat is released.

Of course, it is difficult, maybe impossible, to prove or disprove these theories. As scientists continue to gather new information, other theories may be proposed. The answer may even lie in a combination of them all.

Name _____   Date _____

For the student:

1. Why can't scientists drill into the Earth's core? _____

_____

2. What are seismic waves? _____

_____

3. What is an important difference in the behavior of P-waves and S-waves traveling through liquids?

_____

4. Why do scientists believe the outer core is liquid? _____

_____

5. Why do scientists believe the inner core is solid? _____

_____

6. What do scientists think is the temperature in the Earth's core? _____

7. If you take a hot apple pie out of the oven, the air in the room will eventually cool the crust. What might have cooled the surface of the Earth?

_____

8. As you go deeper into the Earth, temperatures increase. How might this fact support the second theory?

_____

9. If the third theory is correct, what might happen to the Earth's temperature if the radioactive material were to all completely decompose?

_____

10. Why can't scientists prove any of these theories? _____

_____

The Continental Drift Theory

In the early 1900s, a German scientist studied the outlines of the Earth's landmasses. Alfred Wegener believed that the landmasses could all fit together. In 1915 he published a book explaining his continental drift theory.

Wegener believed that 200 million years ago the Earth was one large land mass, which he called Pangaea, meaning All Earth. His theory stated that the large continent split up and the pieces drifted apart from each other, eventually forming the continents as we know them today.

Wegener's theory was not well received and was generally not accepted. He did not seem to have enough hard evidence or proof to support his ideas. In the 1960s, however, scientists uncovered new evidence that seemed to support Wegener's theory.

Scientists located a fossil known as Glossopteris, a seed fern which lived 250 million years ago. These fossils were found in South Africa, Australia, and India. Scientists believe that the seeds of this ancient plant were too big to have been carried by wind. They cannot explain how the plant could have traveled the great distances represented by the current placement of the continents.

Other fossil evidence included a swamp-dweller known as Lystrosaurus. This hippo-like reptile is believed to have lived 200 million years ago. Fossil bones have been found in Africa and South America, and teeth have been uncovered in Antarctica. Scientists do not believe this animal would have been able to swim the vast oceans that currently separate these land masses.

Rocks have also provided support for Wegener's theory. The folded Cape Mountains of South Africa correlate with the folded mountains found near Buenos Aires, Argentina. It is very likely they belonged to the same mountain range at one time.

Scientists have also found similar glacial deposits in South America, Africa, India, Australia, and Antarctica. Their findings indicate that the same ice sheet may have covered this entire area during one of the ice ages.

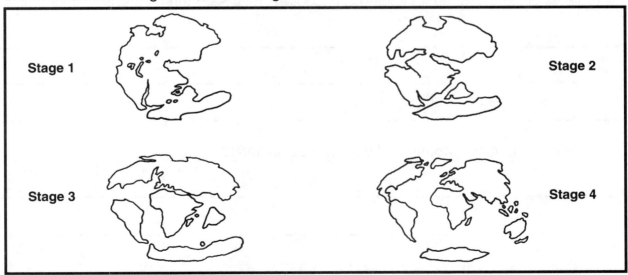

The Continental Drift Theory proposes that there was originally only one large land mass called Pangaea, which began to split up and drift apart until today we have seven continents.

Name _____   Date _____

For the student:

1. What made Wegener believe the continents may have all been one unit?

_____

_____

_____

2. Why wasn't Wegener's theory accepted, initially?

_____

_____

_____

3. How long was it before new evidence emerged to support Wegener's original theory?

_____

_____

_____

4. What was significant about finding Glossopteris fossils on three different continents?

_____

_____

_____

5. What was significant about the Lystrosaurus findings?

_____

_____

_____

Name _____ Date _____

From Pangaea to North America

In the early 1900s, Alfred Wegener published his theory that the Earth's continents had once been a single landmass, had split, and then drifted to their present positions. His theory was generally not accepted until new evidence was uncovered in the 1960s. At that time, his theory was updated and refined.

According to the modern version of the continental drift theory, 800 million years ago Pangaea was the Earth's only continent. It is believed that Pangaea eventually divided into two parts. The northern part has been named Laurasia, and the southern part, Gondwanaland. Eventually, Laurasia divided to become North America, Europe, and Asia. Gondwanaland split up to become South America, Africa, Australia, India, and Antarctica. Scientists believe the continents are still moving, anywhere from 1 to 5 centimeters (.4 to 2 inches) per year.

For the student:

Using the information provided above, write the appropriate name of the land mass in each of the shapes below.

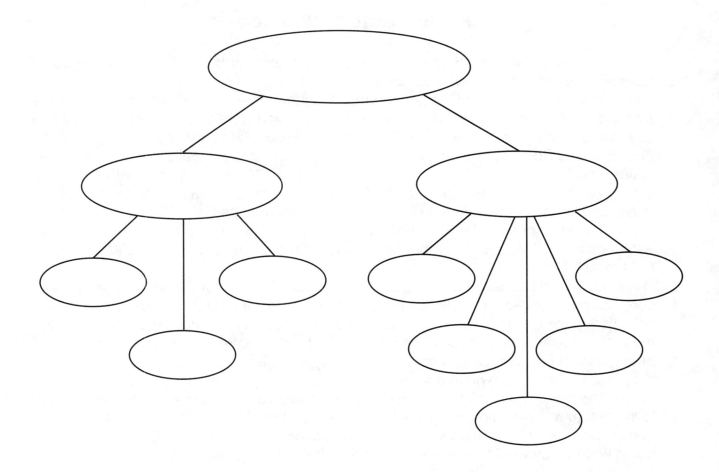

Ocean Floor Spreading

In the 1950s, scientists began studying the ocean floor in detail. Prior to that time they did not have the techniques or the equipment to make the studies possible. With the development of the precision depth recorder and with the use of the Glomar Challenger, a research ship used as a drilling platform, a new frontier was opened.

One of the unexpected discoveries was the presence of underwater mountains. Scientists located mid-ocean ridges, the longest mountain chains in the world. In exploring the ridge areas, they learned that rocks found near the ridges were younger than those that were farther away. They discovered that magma, from deep in the Earth's mantle, was able to rise through vents or cracks in the ridges to add to the ocean floor. From this evidence, scientists were able to determine that new ocean floor was forming and that the ocean floor was spreading.

While the ocean seemed to be forming new crust, and the existing crust was spreading, the Earth's surface was not getting any larger. Nature maintains a balance. To offset the newer, younger crust being formed, older rocks were forced down into the mantle, creating deep valleys and trenches. When the matter was forced deep enough into the mantle, the heat was great enough to make the matter molten once again. The former crust would now, once again, be part of the mantle, and the process could begin again.

Plate Tectonics Theory

The plate tectonics theory explains how the continents drifted and the origins of volcanoes, earthquakes, and mountains.

The Earth's crust and the upper part of the mantle are solid. They are known as the *lithosphere.* The lithosphere is divided into sections called *plates.* Scientists have identified seven major plates and several smaller ones. The major plates are: the Pacific, the North American, the South American, the Eurasian, the African, the Australian, and the Antarctic plates. The Pacific plate is the largest of all, consisting of 20 percent of the Earth's crust. All of these plates, with the exception of the Pacific plate, contain both continental and ocean crust. Smaller plates include the Caribbean and Arabian plates.

The lithosphere sits on the hot, fluid portion of the mantle that is known as the *asthenosphere.* This section of the Earth's interior is believed to be about 200 kilometers (124 miles) thick.

Geologists believe that the plates move about on the asthenosphere because of convection currents deep within the Earth. A convection current is the movement of gases or liquids caused by differences in temperature. Scientists believe that currents rise through the mantle towards mid-ocean ridges. When the molten material meets the rigid material at the lithosphere, it begins to travel horizontally. As the material begins to cool, it turns downward again, returning to the mantle. The cycle is repeated throughout the mantle.

The situation is a bit like a pan of water sitting on a stove burner. The water closest to the burner will warm first. It will rise toward the top, move across the surface of the water, and fall again to the bottom of the pan. If small pieces of wood were floating on the surface of the water, they would move with the flow of the convection current.

Name _____   Date _____

For the student:

1. Why didn't scientists know a lot about the ocean floor prior to the 1950s? _____

_____

2. What did the precision depth recorder help scientists discover?_____

_____

3. What are mid-ocean ridges? _____

_____

4. Why are the rocks close to a mid-ocean ridge younger than the ones that are farther away?

_____

_____

5. If molten matter from the mantle was able to rise through vents in the ridges, why didn't the mantle itself shrink and the thickness of the crust increase?

_____

_____

6. What is the lithosphere? _____

7. What is the asthenosphere? _____

8. How many major plates does the lithosphere have? _____

9. What is the largest plate, and how is it different from all the other plates? _____

_____

10. How are the plates able to move on the asthenosphere?_____

_____

Plate Movement: In, Out, and Sideways

The lithosphere, or solid part of the Earth, is divided into plates. The places where these plates meet are called *plate boundaries.* The plates ride on the asthenosphere, or hot, fluid, upper portion of the mantle. There are three types of movement that seem to occur at the plate boundaries or zones.

The first type of zone is called the *spreading zone.* As the name indicates, this is an area where plates would spread away from each other. Most spreading occurs on the ocean floor, along the mid-ocean ridges. Where this ocean spreading occurs, new ocean crust is formed.

The second type of zone is a *fracture* or *fault zone.* At this meeting place, plates slide past each other. No new Earth matter is created, nor is any lost. Shallow earthquakes may occur at a fracture or fault zone.

The third type of zone is a *converging zone,* where two plates come together. There are two different types of convergence that occur. In the first instance, as the plates meet, one plate slides over the other plate. The lower plate is forced down towards the mantle. This type of convergence may result in the occurrence of deep earthquakes or the formation of volcanoes. In the second type of convergence, the two plates meet, collide, and fold, creating folded mountain ranges.

Which Way Do You Go?

Look carefully at the four drawings below. With the information you have learned about plate movements, identify each of the plate zones pictured: convergent (type 1), convergent (type 2), spreading, and fracture (fault).

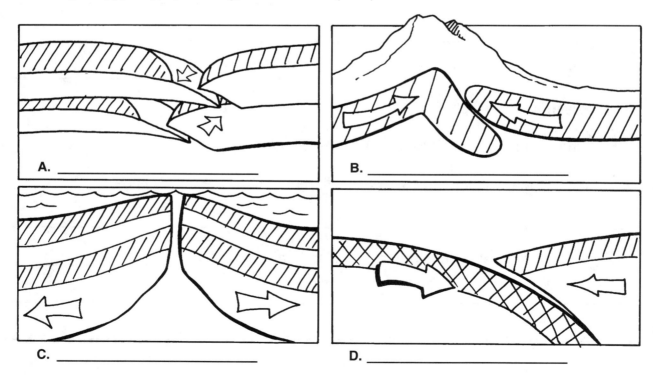

A. _____

B. _____

C. _____

D. _____

Name _____   Date _____

For the student:

1. What are plate boundaries?

_____

_____

2. What happens at a spreading zone?

_____

_____

3. What can happen at a fracture, or fault, zone?

_____

_____

4. In what kind of situation might volcanoes form?

_____

_____

5. How might folded mountains be created?

_____

_____

6. Identify each of the plate zones:

a. _____   b. _____

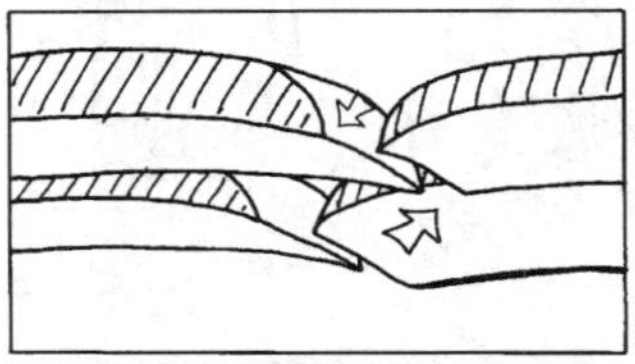

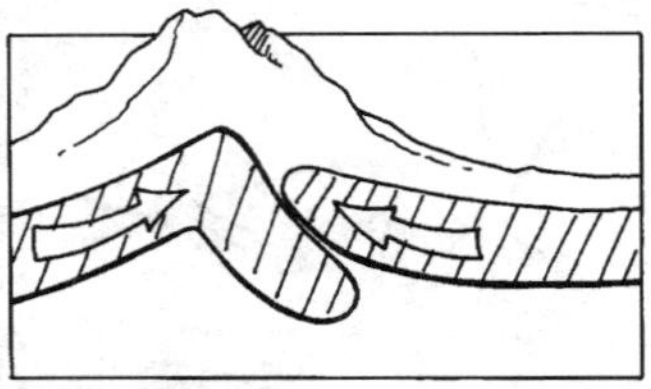

c. _____   d. _____

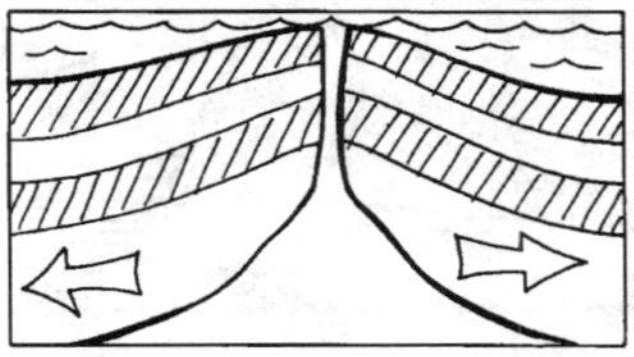

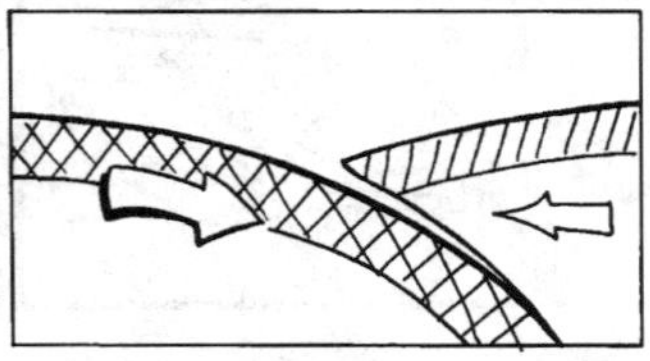

Surface Activity on Earth

Scientists have developed theories regarding the way the Earth was formed. They have also developed models of the structure of our home planet. These theories and models have been the result of indirect observations.

The Earth is a constantly changing sphere. Many of those changes occur right on the surface. These surface activities may be observed, measured, and often reconstructed in laboratories. They can be understood as the result of direct observations.

Earth has been changing for a very long time. Some of the changes are relatively fast, but most changes require a very long time. Scientists believe that the processes that have changed the Earth in the past still exist today; the same processes are at work changing our world now. This idea is known as the *principle of uniformity.*

Weathering is a very important process of surface change. Weathering can be defined as the breaking down of the lithosphere by the action of wind, ice, plants, animals, and chemical changes. Remember that the lithosphere is the solid part of Earth. Weathering is a very slow process. It is also a continuous process. It affects all substances that are exposed to the atmosphere.

Agents of weathering include wind, ice, plants, animals, and chemical changes.

Name _____   Date _____

For the student:

1. What is the principle of uniformity?

_____

_____

_____

2. What is weathering?

_____

_____

_____

3. What is the lithosphere?

_____

_____

_____

4. Does weathering ever stop? Why or why not?

_____

_____

_____

5. What is affected by weathering?

_____

_____

_____

Mechanical Weathering

Weathering is the process of breaking down the lithosphere by wind, water, ice, plants, animals, or chemical change. There are two kinds of weathering: mechanical and chemical.

Mechanical weathering is the process of breaking down rock into smaller pieces. The makeup of the rock is not altered, only its size. There are five different ways that mechanical weathering can occur.

Temperature can produce mechanical weathering. During the day, the sun's energy heats a rock's surface. The internal temperature does not change. During the night, the rock's surface will cool. The following day, the heating and cooling begins again. The repeated change from hot to cold may cause the rock to peel or flake layers that are parallel to the rock's surface. This peeling or flaking is known as *exfoliation.*

A second type of mechanical weathering may be caused by frost. Water may enter a small crack or hole in a rock. As temperatures drop to freezing, the water will expand. As the water expands, it will make a larger crack or hole in the rock. When the water melts, it may move deeper into the bottom of the crack or hole and refreeze. Eventually the rock will break into pieces. The repeated freezing and melting is known as *ice wedging.* We are familiar with the effects of ice wedging—cracks in roads and potholes.

The third type of mechanical weathering is *organic activity.* This may be in the form of tree roots growing in a crack in a rock. As the tree grows and the roots expand, they will pry material loose. This is known as *root-pry.* Animals burrowing homes, such as ants, worms, and woodchucks, also contribute to organic weathering. People may also be responsible for organic weathering by digging, cutting stone, or even driving on roads.

Gravity is the fourth type of mechanical weathering. Landslides move downhill due to the force of gravity. As the rocks cascade down, they collide and break into smaller pieces.

The last type of mechanical weathering is called *abrasion*, which is the wearing away by solid particles carried by wind, water, or other forces. Wind-blown sand is an abrasive that will weather even some of the hardest rocks.

Mechanical weathering can be caused by exfoliation, ice wedging, gravity, organic activity, and abrasion.

Chemical Weathering

Remember that weathering is the process of breaking down the lithosphere by wind, water, ice, plants, animals, or chemical change. There are two kinds of weathering: mechanical and chemical.

While mechanical weathering alters only the size of the rocks, chemical weathering alters the mineral composition, or the chemical makeup, of the rocks as well. There are three different kinds of chemical weathering.

Oxidation is the first type of chemical weathering. This is a process combining oxygen with another substance. The end result is the creation of an entirely new substance. An example of oxidation is the combination of iron and oxygen to form rust. If a material is colored differently on the inside than the outside, it is an indication that oxidation may be taking place.

The second type of chemical weathering is *carbonation*. When carbon dioxide dissolves in water, carbonic acid is formed. This acid reacts with other substances, creating chemical changes. An example is found with acid rain, created when carbon dioxide dissolves in rain water. Acid rain will dissolve some kinds of rocks. More evidence of the effect of carbonic acid can be seen in Mammoth Cave and Carlsbad Cavern, both formed by this process when rain water seeped underground.

The final type of chemical weathering is caused by plant acids, known as *humic acids.* Mosses and lichens provide a good example. As these plants grow on rocks, they produce acids that, in turn, break down the minerals found within the rocks.

Humic acids produced by plants and carbonic acids produced when carbon dioxide dissolves in water can break down rocks and are important agents of chemical weathering.

Name _____   Date _____

For the student:

1. What is mechanical weathering? _____

_____

2. What is exfoliation? _____

_____

3. What is ice wedging? _____

_____

4. What is root-pry? _____

_____

5. What is an example of mechanical weathering by gravity? _____

_____

6. How does chemical weathering differ from mechanical weathering? _____

_____

_____

7. What type of weathering produces rust? _____

_____

8. How is acid rain formed? _____

_____

9. Acid rain is an example of which type of chemical weathering? _____

_____

10. What are humic acids? _____

_____

How Fast Does Weathering Occur?

Weathering is a slow process; however, there are several factors that affect the actual rate of weathering. The first factor is the type of rock that is exposed to the atmosphere. Sandstone is an example of a rock that can weather rapidly. Granite, however, is very resistant to weathering. The condition of the exposed rock is also important. Rocks that have cracks or holes in them to begin with will weather at a faster rate than unblemished rocks.

The second factor that affects weathering is the area's climate. Climate is determined by the amount of precipitation, the temperature, and the geographical location of an area. An area with a great deal of moisture will see the effects of weathering, both mechanical and chemical, faster than a dry area.

Pollution is the final factor affecting the rate of weathering. The burning of fossil fuels releases carbon dioxide into the air, polluting the environment. As more carbon dioxide is released into the air, more carbonation can occur, creating more acids to weather the area's rocks.

With the information you have already learned, it should be easy to conclude that tropical climates will have the fastest rate of weathering. The temperatures are high, the air is moist, and there is an abundance of plant material. Deserts will have one of the slowest rates because of the lack of humidity, or water in the air. In temperate climates, summer is a time of faster weathering because of the higher temperatures. However, alternate freezing and thawing associated with winter and early spring also have a noticeable effect.

Tropical climates have the fastest rates of weathering, while deserts have the slowest rates.

Name _____   Date _____

For the student:

1. What are examples of rocks that are easily weathered and rocks that are resistant to weathering?

_____

_____

_____

2. Why is the condition of a rock an important factor?

_____

_____

_____

3. What climate is the most conducive to rapid weathering?

_____

_____

_____

4. Burning fossil fuels creates air pollution. How does this affect the rate of weathering?

_____

_____

_____

5. Why is a desert an area of slow weathering?

_____

_____

_____

Name_____   Date _____

Weathering: A Graphic Organizer

The boxes below have been set up to help you organize the information about weathering. This can serve as a study guide. Complete the chart by adding the labels in their correct boxes.

Weathering	Frost	Gravity
Types of Weathering	Carbonation	Abrasion
Temperature	Plant Acids	Mechanical
Oxidation	Organic Activity	Chemical
Rate of Weathering	Climate	Type of rock
	Pollution	

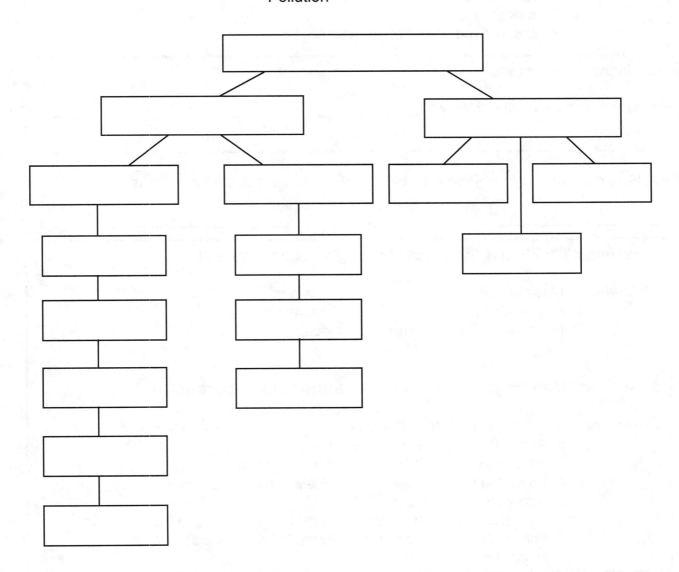

Geology

Name _____   Date _____

Weathering Experiments

Experiment #1: What is the effect of cold temperatures?

Materials: baby food jar   grease pencil
               plastic bag   ruler

Procedure: 1. Half fill the baby food jar with water.
             2. Mark the water line with a grease pencil.
             3. Measure the height of the line; record.
             4. Put the jar in the plastic bag.
             5. Carefully place the jar and bag in the freezer.
             6. Remove the jar after the water has frozen.
             7. Mark the ice line.
             8. Measure the height of the line; record.

Understanding the results:

1. Which line was higher? Why? _____

_____

2. How do your results compare to water that freezes in the cracks of rocks? _____

_____

Experiment #2: What is the effect of changing temperatures?

Materials: glass marble   oven mitt
               heavy saucepan   metal bowl
               hot plate or Bunsen burner   ice
               tongs

* Caution: Use goggles when performing this experiment!

Procedure: 1. Place the marble in the saucepan.
             2. Add water until the pan is half full.
             3. Heat the water, with the marble, until it boils.
             4. While the water is heating, put the ice in the metal bowl.
             5. Add water until the bowl is half full.
             6. After the water in the pan has begun boiling, remove the marble.
             7. Immediately place the marble in the bowl of ice water.
             8. Record the results.

Understanding the results:

1. What effect did the change of temperature have on the marble? _____

_____

2. How do your results compare to the effect of temperature change on rocks? _____

_____

Experiment #3: What is the effect of oxidation?

Materials: steel wool
               dry, clean sand
               large tray

Procedure: 1. Place the sand in the tray
               2. Place the steel wool in the tray.
               3. Wet the sand and the steel wool.
               4. Observe the sand and steel wool immediately.
               5. Record your results.
               6. Observe the sand and steel wool after 24 hours, 48 hours, and 72 hours.
               7. Record your results.

Understanding the results:

1. What happened to the sand and the steel wool immediately?_____

_____

2. What happened to the sand and the steel wool after 24 hours? 48 hours? 72 hours?

_____

_____

3. What caused the changes?_____

_____

4. How is this similar to changes caused by nature?_____

_____

Erosion and Deposition

Weathering is the process that breaks down rock into smaller pieces. There are several different ways in which this can occur. Once the weathering process has occurred, other processes take over.

Erosion is the process of carrying away weathered material. The agents of erosion include moving water, ice, waves, and wind. *Deposition* is the process of laying the weathered material down in a new location.

Most of the time, erosion is a gradual process. It may take millions of years for the agents of erosion to make noticeable differences in the Earth's surface. The Grand Canyon in Arizona is the result of close to three million years of erosion.

Erosion, however, can also act very rapidly. An unusually rainy period can cause rivers to overflow their banks and flood the areas surrounding them. The erosion caused by the rapid rivers and their flooding action can have very quick, devastating results for the Earth's surface and especially for its inhabitants.

In the next few pages, we will look at moving water, ice, waves, and wind as the agents of erosion. We will see how each agent works. We will also investigate the effects of deposition by each of these agents.

For three million years, the process of erosion has been creating the Grand Canyon.

Name _____   Date _____

For the student:

1. Write a good definition for each of these words:

    weathering _____

    _____

    erosion _____

    _____

    deposition _____

    _____

2. What are three agents of erosion?

    _____

    _____

3. What evidence do scientists have that erosion works slowly over long periods of time?

    _____

    _____

4. What is an example of erosion that works very rapidly?

    _____

    _____

5. What are some devastating results of a flood for the area's inhabitants?

    _____

    _____

    _____

Agent H₂O: Water
Assignment: Runoff

When water returns to Earth as precipitation, there are several things that can happen to the water. First, it may evaporate back into the atmosphere. Second, it may sink into the ground. Third, the water may be used by plants and animals. Finally, the water may become runoff.

Nearly 40 percent of all precipitation becomes runoff. Runoff is a powerful agent of change because the water carries weathered particles with it, eroding the area. Even large, heavy particles may be dragged along. As they move, the large pieces may, in turn, break down more particles to be carried away.

The amount of runoff formed by precipitation depends on several factors. First, the amount of rainfall affects the runoff; during heavy rains there is greater runoff. Also, areas with high average annual precipitation will be affected more by runoff.

Another factor affecting the amount of runoff is the shape of the land. Very steep slopes will have greater runoff. The water will also be moving at a faster pace. Because of the greater speed, less water will be able to soak into the ground. Flat areas will, naturally, be less affected by runoff.

The type of surface is an important factor, too. Very porous surfaces will have less runoff because more of the water is absorbed into the surface. Impermeable surfaces do not allow much penetration, so they are more affected by runoff.

The amount of plant growth in the area is another factor. Plant roots are able to hold on to the soil. The roots also absorb some of the water for their own life processes. Areas with lush plant growth are less likely to be adversely affected by runoff. Bare ground, however, will show the results of runoff very quickly.

Finally, temperature affects the amount of runoff as well. When temperatures are very warm, evaporation takes care of much of the precipitation, so there is little runoff. When temperatures are very cold, precipitation is trapped in the form of snow or ice, so there is little immediate runoff. Thawing also has a great effect. When thawing occurs slowly, there is less runoff. When thawing occurs rapidly, there is too much water to be absorbed at once, and runoff can be a significant problem.

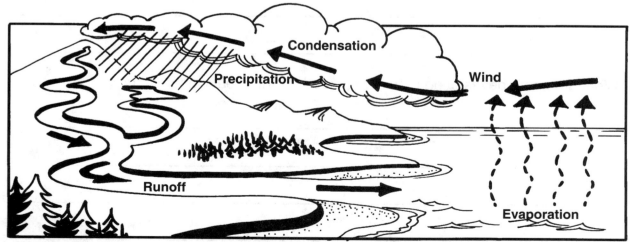

The Water Cycle

Agent H₂O: Water; Assignment: Rivers

Rivers are important agents of erosion. They may be responsible for the greatest amount of erosion because they cover a very large area of the Earth's surface.

Rivers often form in high elevations, usually in the mountains. Due to gravity, water will flow from higher elevations to lower elevations. Runoff at the top of the mountain will begin moving down the mountain, using the areas of the surface that offer the least resistance. The runoff repeatedly uses the same path, eventually forming a channel. As the runoff continues to use the same channel, carrying bits of Earth material with it, the channel deepens and the water moves faster. After a period of time, a stream is formed. Streams begin to flow together, forming rivers. The rivers continue to carry weathered materials, or sediments. The amount of sediment carried by an individual river is determined by the velocity, or speed, of the river and the amount of water it holds.

Scientists classify young rivers as immature. The characteristics of immature rivers include a steep-sided valley that forms a V. The water moves quickly, and rapids or waterfalls are not uncommon. Immature rivers experience a lot of erosion quickly. Large particles of sediment are moved rapidly down the river.

Older rivers are classified as mature and have their own characteristics. They have an eroded valley floor, with the sides of the valley often quite distant from the present riverbed. Mature rivers are often curvy, as they meander through the river valley. The water moves more slowly, carrying smaller particles of sediment. Erosion continues to be an active process, but at a much slower pace.

The sediments carried by a river are referred to as the *river load.* The load consists of two parts: the *suspended load* and the *bed load.* The suspended load consists of the small particles or rock materials that are dispersed throughout the water and easily carried downstream. The bed load consists of the larger particles that are dragged and bounced along near the bottom of the river.

A large, fast-moving river will look quite muddy because it is carrying a heavy load. As a river slows, some of the materials settle out and the load is lighter, leaving the water looking clearer. Large particles tend to settle out directly on the riverbed. Smaller particles may settle where the river bends or curves. The force of the moving water will erode the outside section of a bend and deposit sediments on the slower, inside section of the bend.

As an aging river continues to meander, it may form an oxbow lake. The process begins when the meandering forms a U in the river. The action of the water continues to erode the outside of the two curves until the U forms a loop, leaving an island of land in the center of the loop. Deposits begin to build up on either side of the island because the faster water is now by-passing that area. Eventually these areas will fill in completely and a lake will be formed, separated from the main line of the river.

Deposition by a river can also form a delta. When a moving river flows into standing water, such as a lake or ocean, it slows down rapidly. It is no longer able to carry all of the material in its load, so it deposits large amounts of sediment. The sediments build up to form a delta, often spreading out into the lake or ocean.

Rivers are also responsible for building up floodplains. When the water level in a mature river increases, it may overflow the banks of the river on both sides. When these flood waters leave the river, they slow down and deposit the large amounts of sediment they were carrying. These sediments build up to form rich, fertile soil that is often used for farming.

37

Name _____   Date _____

For the student:

1. What is precipitation? _____

_____

2. What happens to nearly half the precipitation after it leaves the atmosphere? _____

_____

3. How does climate affect the amount of runoff? _____

_____

4. How does the structure of an area affect the amount of runoff? _____

_____

5. How do the listed factors affect the amount of runoff in your area? _____

_____

6. What role does gravity play in the formation of a river? _____

_____

7. What is sediment? _____

_____

8. What two factors decide how much sediment a river can carry? _____

_____

9. What is the difference between a river's suspended load and its bed load? _____

_____

10. What are three characteristics that differentiate an immature river and a mature river?

_____

_____

Moments in History
A Great Flood

As a geologist, Dr. Victor Baker of the University of Arizona in Tucson has been doing research into Earth's history. He believes that the greatest flood ever may have taken place towards the end of the Ice Age.

About 16,000 years ago, a huge ice sheet covered the area that is now known as Siberia. The ice sheet began to melt as climatic changes occurred across the planet. As the glacier melted and retreated, great pieces of ice broke loose. These ice slabs formed temporary dams on the lakes and rivers in the mountainous regions.

The great glacier continued to melt, and water built up behind these new dams. The pressure from the water pushing against the dams continued to mount until finally the dams couldn't resist the pressure any more. The dams broke, and thousands of liters of water went surging across the countryside.

Baker and his associates believe the floodwaters blanketed the land with water up to 485 meters (1,600 feet) deep. That is deeper than the deepest of our Great Lakes, Lake Superior. They believe the flood was 65 times greater than the worst flood ever recorded along the Amazon River, the largest river on Earth.

In order to come to this conclusion, the geologists went to Siberia and studied deep channels and other surface features that were created by the flood's erosion. They were able to feed information from their observations into computers and reconstruct the actions of this great flood, a moment in history that had gone unnoticed until now.

Agent Freezeout: Glaciers
Assignment: Poles and Mountains

Glaciers are important agents of erosion; however, they are not the leaders in their effectiveness. They carry a more massive load than rivers do, but they cover a smaller area and do their work over a shorter period of time.

What, exactly, are glaciers? They are large masses of moving ice and snow. They are found in areas where there is a great deal of snowfall that does not melt from winter to winter. Scientists have identified two basic types of glaciers: valley glaciers and continental glaciers. Let's see how they differ.

Valley glaciers form in mountains, high in old river valleys. Elevations are high enough and temperatures are low enough that snow, which falls during the winter and early spring, does not melt. It builds up from year to year and slowly turns to ice. Eventually, with the help of gravity, the weight of the ice begins to move the glacier down the mountain valley. Valley glaciers are also known as alpine glaciers.

Continental glaciers form in the polar regions of the planet. They form large sheets of ice that may cover millions of square kilometers. Once again, snowfall does not melt, but accumulates. The weight of the piled snow pushes down on the glacier, moving it out from the center. (Try forming a mound of clay. Put it on a table and push down on the center with your hand. The clay will "squish" out, moving along the edges.) Continental glaciers are sometimes referred to as ice caps and are currently found primarily in Greenland and Antarctica.

The Earth material carried by a glacier is known as the *glacial load.* It consists of both large and small particles of debris. Unlike a river load, the glacial load does not separate by size.

There are three ways that glaciers gather or move Earth materials. They push and carry debris in front of them as they move down the valley or across the land. They also pluck debris from the land beneath them. It becomes frozen in the ice and moves along under the glacier. Finally, the glaciers loosen debris from the valley walls as they scrape through the area.

A valley before (left) and after (right) a glacier has moved through.

Agent Freezeout: Glaciers
Assignment: Destroy and Create

As agents of erosion, glaciers wear down land surfaces. The debris that is frozen underneath the glacier serves as an abrasive. It grinds and polishes the surfaces that the glacier drags across.

The erosive effect of a valley glacier is very similar to that of a river. Most notably, as an alpine glacier moves through an area, it erodes the V-shaped valley into a U-shaped valley, often leaving shear walls on either side.

Glaciers are also important agents of deposition. As the front end of a glacier moves into a warmer area, the ice begins to melt. The glacier continues to move, but it melts faster than it moves. At this point, scientists say a glacier is retreating. As the ice melts, it drops its load. Rocks, clay, and other debris are deposited, often great distances from where they were originally formed.

All material deposited by a glacier is known as *glacial drift.* Drift, however, may be subdivided according to how it is deposited. If the drift is directly deposited by the glacier, it is called *till.* Till is not sorted by water action, so it is a mixture of sizes. If the drift is first carried away by water and then deposited, it is called *outwash.* Outwash is sorted by size and deposited in layers.

Glaciers are responsible for forming several different landscape features. Moraines are ridges of till deposited by glaciers. Terminal moraines form at the front edge of the glacier. Lateral moraines form along the sides. Studying the contents of moraines helps scientists understand where the glaciers formed. The locations of the moraines help them understand the extent of the glacier's movement.

Meltwater is formed when glacial ice melts. Meltwater may form a stream, carrying away sand and gravel from the glacier. The meltwater stream may erode a channel and deposit outwash debris in layers, similar to a river's erosion and deposition. Meltwater may also form a sheet of water. This meltwater forms a fan-shaped area in front of a terminal moraine. The outwash is deposited across the area, forming a fertile plain. Many outwash plains are now used for farming.

Glaciers may also form lakes. As deposits pile up in low areas, they may block rivers and trap the water. This trapped water will form a lake covering much of the lowland area. Another type of lake is formed when blocks of ice are left behind as the glacier moves. The ice blocks become covered with debris and they melt slowly. When the melting occurs, the debris on top of the water sinks into the hole, and a kettle lake is formed.

Icebergs can also be formed by glaciers. Sometimes as glaciers move, they may reach the sea. Pieces of ice break off and float away. These are icebergs and are most commonly found near Greenland and Antarctica. The icebergs contain rock debris gathered by the glacier. When the iceberg begins to melt, the debris settles to the ocean floor, many miles from where the rocks were formed.

Geology

Agent Freezeout: Glaciers; Assignment: Poles and Mountains
Agent Freezeout: Glaciers; Assignment: Destroy and Create

Name _____   Date _____

For the student:

1. What is a glacier? _____

_____

2. Where are alpine glaciers found?_____

_____

3. What is an ice cap? _____

_____

4. What causes valley glaciers to move? _____

_____

5. In what direction do continental glaciers move? _____

_____

6. What is a retreating glacier? _____

_____

7. What is the difference between a terminal moraine and a lateral moraine? _____

_____

8. Why would scientists want to study glacial moraines? _____

_____

9. What is the difference between till and outwash? _____

_____

10. How are kettle lakes formed?_____

_____

Agent Splishsplash: Waves
Assignment: From Sea to Shining Sea

Waves are curving swells of water caused by wind, tides, and even earthquakes. They move along the surface of the water. They are another powerful agent of change. The size and strength of waves often depend on the winds moving them. Strong winds will create large waves; lighter breezes will produce smaller swells.

Waves reshape the shoreline, which is the area where a body of water meets land. The rate of erosion depends on several factors. The size of the wave is important, as is the force of the wave. A normal wave can erode the shoreline at a rate of 1 to 1.5 centimeters (.4 to .6 inch) per year. Weather conditions greatly affect the rate of erosion. Severe, stormy weather may increase the rate to as much as 25 meters (82 feet) per day! The type of rock, or earth material, along the shoreline is also an important factor. Loose, fragile soils will be eroded faster than large blocks of dense rock.

As waves move near the shoreline, their movement begins to slow down. Gravity pulls at the crests of the waves and they tumble over, forming the surf. This breaking action of the waves fragments the rocks beneath it. The water picks up rock material and carries it toward the shore as suspended pieces of rock and other debris. When the waves hit the shoreline, these suspended particles fragment the rocks along the shoreline.

The action of the waves also pushes water into cracks and holes along the shore. The abrasive action of the particles in the water makes the cracks and holes larger. The process continues until the cracks and holes become large enough to break the rocks into pieces that fall along the shoreline or into the water.

Waves are constantly eroding the shoreline.

Agent Splishsplash: Waves
Assignment: Beaches, Bars, and Spits

Wave action is responsible for eroding the shoreline. As this process takes place, several different kinds of features may form.

When waves pound into cliffs (steep faces of rock along the shoreline), the bottoms of the cliffs begin to wear away. As the base of the cliff recedes, the top may break off and fall into the sea. There the action of the waves may grind the rocks into sand and silt. This area is called a terrace, a flat platform at the base of a cliff. The terrace will slow down the action of the waves, slowing the rate of erosion.

Some of the rocks along a cliff may be resistant to the action of the waves. They do not wear away or fall over, forming a terrace. They remain standing while the rocks around them erode. These tall islands of rock are called *stacks.*

Sometimes part of a sea cliff will have less resistant material than the rest of the cliff. This area will erode first, forming a hollowed-out area, or a cave. If the waves are able to wear away the rock through the back side of the cave, an *arch* may be formed.

When the waves erode the landforms, they move the earth material to other places. The deposition of these particles may form other interesting features along the shoreline. One with which most of us are familiar is a *beach.* Beaches are formed when the eroded particles are deposited parallel to the shore. They may be made of finely ground sand or large pebbles. They may be formed from material brought by the waves from nearby shorelines. They may also be formed by materials deposited by rivers and streams and then carried along by waves.

The color of a beach may give some indication as to the types of material from which it was formed. Beaches along the Atlantic coast of the U.S. are often white, sandy beaches. Most of them are formed from eroded quartz. In Hawaii, the black beaches are made of weathered volcanic rock. Other beaches may be made of shell or coral materials.

Most of the time, waves do not come straight at the shoreline. They come in at an angle. The waves turn the water so it runs parallel to the shoreline. This is known as a *longshore current.* If the shoreline bends, the longshore current may deposit its material in the open ocean. The material will build up over time, forming a *sandbar.* If the sandbar is connected to the shoreline, it is known as a *spit.*

The eroding action of waves can create several different rock and land formations.

Geology

Agent Splishsplash: Waves; Assignment: From Sea to Shining Sea
Agent Splishsplash: Waves; Assignment: Beaches, Bars, and Spits

Name _____   Date _____

For the student:

1. What is a wave? _____

_____

2. What are four factors that affect a wave's rate of erosion? _____

_____

3. What two factors cause waves to break near the shoreline? _____

_____

4. When waves enter small cracks and holes in rocks along the shoreline, what happens to the rocks?

_____

_____

5. What kind of weathering is that? _____

6. What are three cliff features that may be formed by wave erosion? _____

_____

7. What is a beach? _____

_____

8. Why are beaches different colors in different areas? _____

_____

9. Why do the size and shape of beaches change? _____

_____

10. What is a spit? _____

_____

Agent Blowhard: Wind
Assignment: Deflation

Wind is moving air. It is not a very effective agent of erosion on its own. Wind is not dense enough to carry much material. It does, however, affect the Earth's landscape by blowing away loose material and by carrying abrasive particles. Let's look a bit closer at the work of the wind.

Deflation is the process of removing loose material from the surface of the land. Wind is most effective in dry areas that do not have much vegetation to hold the soil and other matter in place. Exposed areas such as deserts, beaches, and plowed fields are vulnerable to the wind's deflation.

The wind is able to pick up loose matter as it blows over an area. Most windblown matter is clay, silt, dust, and sand. The finer particles travel several meters up above the ground. The larger particles remain within a few centimeters of the surface and are frequently bounced and rolled along. All of these particles are abrasive, polishing rocks and pebbles as they bump into them.

Since larger windblown particles remain fairly close to the ground, most erosion occurs close to the ground. In desert areas it is not uncommon to see telephone poles surrounded by piles of rock at the base. The piles may be a meter tall. The rocks protect the more easily eroded wooden poles from wind damage.

The amount of damage done by wind depends on several different factors. The size of the particles and the speed of the wind are important. Smaller particles are less damaging, and mild winds do not blow the particles against objects with as much force. The length of time during which the wind blows is also important. The amount of resistance offered by the object is a final determining factor.

Several landscape features may be formed by the erosive action of the wind. Wind caves may form when less resistant materials are eroded and more resistant materials remain. If the wind is able to go all the way through the back wall of the cave, a wind bridge or arch may form. This type of erosion is usually a gradual process, taking a long time.

Areas with exposed, loose material, such as deserts, are greatly affected by deflation.

Agent Blowhard: Wind
Assignment: Tell Me How It's Dune

Wind is able to pick up particles of dust, sand, silt, and clay. The amount of material carried by the wind depends on the speed of the wind. Faster winds are able to carry more material. (This is similar to the load carried by water; faster water can carry a heavier load.)

When the wind encounters a barrier of some kind, it slows down. When the wind slows down, it cannot carry as much material. It drops the material at the base of the barrier. People have taken advantage of this idea and erected windbreaks, or barriers against the wind. Fences are effective to some extent. Plants, trees, and shrubs are even better at stopping the wind and protecting crops and buildings.

There are natural barriers to the wind as well. Along beaches, grasses, bushes, and large rocks may be windbreaks. In the deserts, trees, sagebrush, and rocks serve the same purpose. The wind drops its load at the foot of the windbreak. Each time that is done, the deposits build up a bit more. Finally, the deposits themselves help slow the wind. Eventually, the deposits build up enough to form dunes.

Sand dunes vary in size and in shape. In general, however, the windward side develops a gentle slope. The wind blows along this slope to the crest, or top, of the dune. Once it reaches the top, the wind dumps its load on the leeward side. The deposits slide down the back side, forming a steep slope. This side is known as the *slipface* of the dune.

Dunes are not fixed features. They move with the wind. The windward side continues to be eroded. The leeward side continues to build up. Dunes have been known to move and completely cover existing structures such as buildings.

An oasis is an interesting feature of the desert. To form an oasis, the area must be eroded to a depth where water is present. Water allows vegetation to grow. The vegetation, in turn, prevents further erosion. Thus, a lush, green island exists in the middle of a barren wasteland.

Loess is fertile soil created by wind deposition. Fine sand and silt from dry riverbeds and glacial lakebeds may not form dunes. Instead, it may be carried to an area farther away. When it is deposited by the wind, it builds up, creating an environment where vegetation can readily grow. The north and central portions of the Mississippi River Valley have rich loess deposits, as do northeast China and the Gobi Desert in Asia.

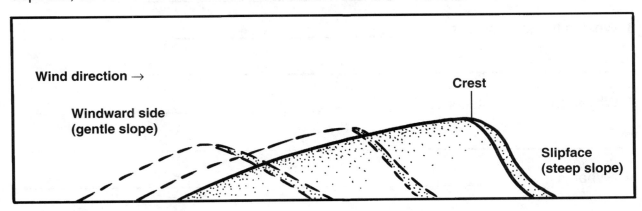

The movement of a sand dune

Name _____ Date _____

For the student:

1. What is wind?_____

_____

2. Is wind as damaging as water? Why or why not? _____

_____

3. Why aren't large particles of matter carried as high in the wind as the smaller ones are?

_____

_____

4. Why are rocks piled up around telephone poles in some desert areas?_____

_____

5. What kind of weathering is wind erosion? _____

_____

6. What is the purpose of a wind break? _____

_____

7. What are some effective wind breaks? _____

_____

8. What is the slipface of a dune? _____

_____

9. Why aren't dunes stationary? _____

_____

10. What is loess?_____

_____

Subsurface Activity: Mountains

Our planet is constantly changing. Natural processes may alter the surface structures and landscape features. Most of the changes are gradual and are hardly noticed. Some of the changes are rapid and have an important impact on people and their daily lives.

Beneath the surface, changes are occurring as well. Once again, most of the changes are gradual and go unnoticed. Some of them, however, are very sudden and can change our lives. We will examine three types of internal changes and their impacts: mountain formation, earthquakes, and volcanoes. Let's begin with mountains.

Most mountains are formed by internal, or subsurface, activities. Volcanic, folded, fault block, and dome mountains are examples. A fifth type of mountain, eroded, is formed by the surface activities of wind and water erosion.

Volcanic mountains are formed when magma—molten rock—is forced out through the crust. It hardens on the Earth's surface and forms a mountain in one of two ways. The first way is through a quiet lava flow. The second type of formation involves an explosion. The magma is held just inside the crust, pressure builds, and finally the molten rock blasts its way onto the surface. Mauna Loa, in Hawaii, is an example of a volcanic mountain.

Folded mountains are the most common type of mountain. There are many well-known examples: the Alps, the Himalayas, the Urals, the Rockies, and the Appalachians. In the early stages of formation, thick deposits of sediment form along the edge of a continent. As the deposits build up, the crust beneath them sinks toward the mantle. The rate of sinking equals the rate of deposition. As the crust and sediments get buried deeper, the pressure and temperature increase. The sediments begin to twist, turn, and fold beneath the pressure. They look a bit like a wave. The upward folds are known as *anticlines,* and the downward folds are *synclines.* Finally, a tremendous force pushes the folded layers up. Geologists believe the force may be caused by the collision of two lithospheric plates. They continue pushing until mountains have been formed. This process takes millions of years.

The third type of mountains are fault block mountains, like the Sierra Nevadas in Utah and Nevada. Geologists believe the Earth's crust bends in as it floats on the fluid-like mantle. It continues bending until the pressure becomes too great, and then the rocks forming the crust split. This area is known as a *fault.* Pressures beneath the fault area continue to push upwards. The rocks move with the pressure, but not as a single unit. The middle section may move higher than the areas on its sides, forming a mountain with two steep sides. The sides may move up, leaving the middle section lower. Once again, the mountains may have steep edges on both sides. Another possibility is that one side will move up at an angle over the other. This forms a mountain with one gently sloping side and one steep side.

A fourth type of mountain is a dome mountain. In its formation, magma is trapped in a pocket beneath the rock layers and is unable to work its way to the surface. The pressure of the magma pushes up the layers of rock, forming a rounded mountain shape. The Black Hills of South Dakota are believed to be dome mountains.

The final type of mountain is not formed by internal activity. Instead, these mountains are formed by erosion. *Plateaus* are flat areas that have been pushed above sea level by forces within the Earth, or have been formed by layers of lava. They are often found near folded mountains. As years pass, streams and rivers erode valleys through the plateau, leaving mountains standing between the valleys. The Catskills and Pike's Peak are examples of eroded mountains.

Name _____   Date _____

For the student:

1. How are volcanic mountains formed?

_____

_____

2. What is the most common type of mountain?

_____

_____

3. How does plate movement affect the formation of folded mountains?

_____

_____

4. How are fault lines important in the formation of fault block mountains?

_____

_____

5. How were each of these mountains formed?

    Catskills _____

    Sierra Nevadas _____

    Mauna Loa _____

    Rockies _____

    Black Hills _____

Name _____   Date _____

Mountains
Their Formation

The drawings below show four ways that mountains can form. Identify each formation as dome, folded, fault block, or eroded. Then provide the name of a mountain or mountain chain for each type of formation.

A. Type _____
   Example _____

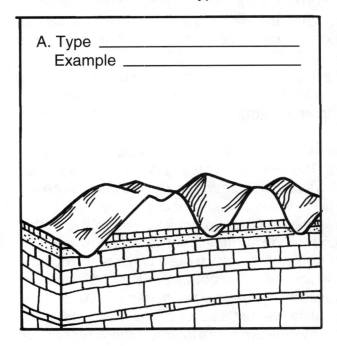

B. Type _____
   Example _____

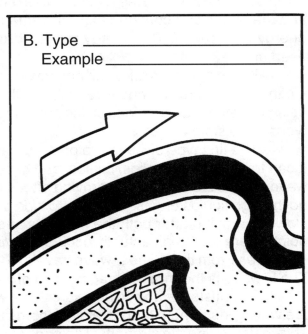

C. Type _____
   Example _____

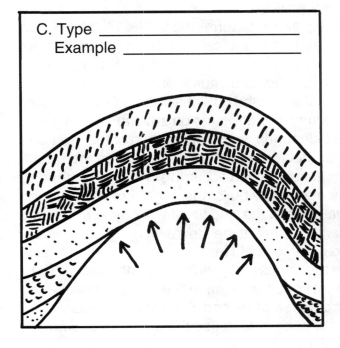

D. Type _____
   Example _____

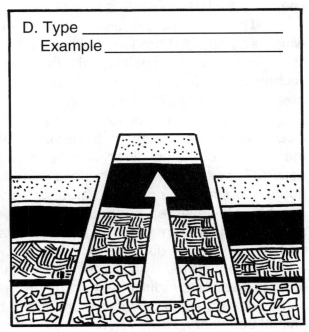

The Moving Earth: Earthquakes

An earthquake is a trembling or shaking of the Earth that occurs because of a sudden movement of the crust. Geologists believe there may be more than one million earthquakes each year.

The most common cause of earthquakes is *faulting.* The lithospheric plates can move in three different directions: away from each other, towards each other, or sliding past each other. When plates slide along, sometimes they catch on each other. Pressure builds up on both sides behind the "catch." When enough pressure builds, the "catch" breaks loose and the plates can continue their movement. When the sliding plates break loose, stored energy is released. The energy travels through the surrounding rocks until the energy is used up.

When energy is released and travels through the rocks, it can do two different things: it can move the rocks, and it can vibrate the rocks. When the rocks vibrate they send out *seismic waves.* Seismologists (scientists who study earthquakes) have identified three types of seismic waves.

The first type of wave is a primary wave or P-wave. This is the fastest type of wave. It can travel through solids, liquids, and gases. The next type of wave is a secondary or S-wave. This is a slower wave, arriving after a P-wave. It can travel through solids but cannot go through liquids or gases. The third type of wave is a surface wave or L-wave. This is the slowest, arriving after both the P-waves and S-waves. This type of wave travels from the point where the break actually occurs, the *focus,* to the surface point directly above it, the *epicenter.* From there, the L-wave travels along the surface, much like a wave on the ocean. The L-wave is the most damaging kind of wave, twisting and bending matter as it travels.

Scientists are able to measure these waves with a *seismograph.* Part of the machine is a writing instrument that carefully records Earth movements as wavy lines. Scientists are able to determine the strength of an earthquake by measuring the height of the waves in the line. Straight lines indicate a lack of earthquake activity.

The magnitude, or strength, of an earthquake is determined by the *Richter Scale,* which is numbered from 1 to 10. Each number on the scale indicates an earthquake 10 times stronger than one associated with the previous number. (So an earthquake of 5.0 on the Richter Scale is ten times stronger than an earthquake measuring 4.0.) Any quake measuring 6.0 or more is considered a major quake with the potential for much destruction.

The actual destruction caused by an earthquake depends on several factors. First, it depends on the strength of the quake. It also depends on the population of the area and the strength of the buildings. Another important factor is the time of day when the quake occurs. For example, an earthquake with a magnitude of 6.0 occurring in the early morning hours in a sparsely populated area with only a few, low buildings might not cause much damage. However, an earthquake of 6.0 occurring in the middle of the day in a densely populated urban area with many tall skyscrapers might be devastating. There would probably be a lot of damage to buildings and great loss of life.

Scientists are trying to develop reliable techniques for predicting earthquakes. They hope to be able to reduce destruction and, most importantly, save lives. There seem to be some warning signs, such as a change in the speed of P- and S-waves and changes in animal behaviors. However, scientists have not been able to use these, or other, warning signals to develop a reliable warning system yet.

Name _____   Date _____

For the student:

1. What are the three types of seismic waves?

_____

_____

_____

2. What is the earthquake's focus?

_____

_____

_____

3. What is the earthquake's epicenter?

_____

_____

_____

4. What does the Richter Scale measure?

_____

_____

_____

5. Much of the damage after an earthquake is caused by fire. How might the fires start?

_____

_____

_____

Earthquakes
The Waves

The top three drawings below demonstrate the three types of seismic waves. The first drawing shows the wave motion of L-waves along the surface. The next drawing demonstrates the vibrating motion caused by P-waves. The final drawing shows the up-and-down movement caused by S-waves.

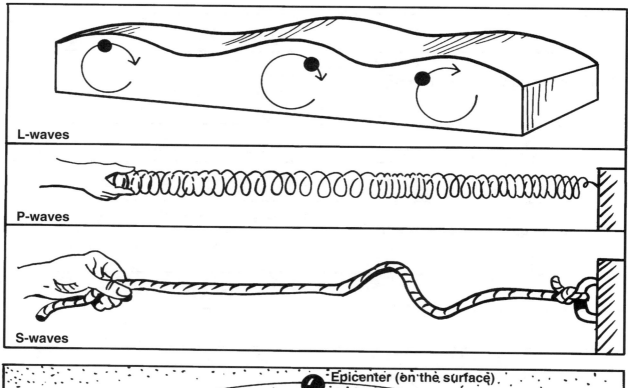

L-waves

P-waves

S-waves

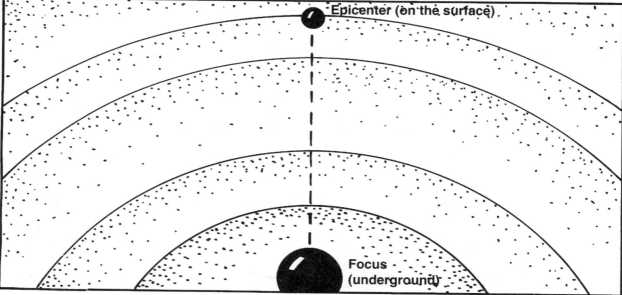

Epicenter (on the surface)

Focus (underground)

The L-wave travels from the focus to the epicenter and then travels along the Earth's surface.

Volcanoes
Mountains of Fire

Volcanoes are mountains from which hot, molten rock bursts. There are three types of volcanoes: cinder cone, shield, and composite cone. Each type of volcano forms in a slightly different way.

Magma is hot, liquid rock beneath the Earth's surface. It is stored in large pockets or chambers. Magma rises from these chambers through cracks in rocks or by melting the rocks above it.

When magma reaches the surface, it is called *lava.* Lava cools as it is exposed to the atmosphere. Repeated eruptions cause lava to build up. Eventually the lava will form a mountain. At the top of the volcano a steep-sided hole, known as a *crater,* may form. The volcano's opening, which allows the magma to flow to the Earth's surface, is called the *vent.*

Different kinds of magma and lava are responsible for different types of volcanic flow. Dark lava is thin and runny. It is able to flow gently from the volcano's vent. Light-colored lava, however, does not contain much water. It tends to harden in the vent, blocking the flow of magma from beneath. Steam and new magma become trapped and build up pressure. When the pressure becomes too great, an explosion occurs.

When a volcano explodes, fragments are blasted into the air. Very fine fragments, up to .25 millimeters in diameter, are known as *volcanic dust. Volcanic ash* is a bit larger, up to 5 millimeters in size. Fragments larger than 5 millimeters are known as *volcanic bombs.* They range in size, with the smaller bombs classified as *cinders.*

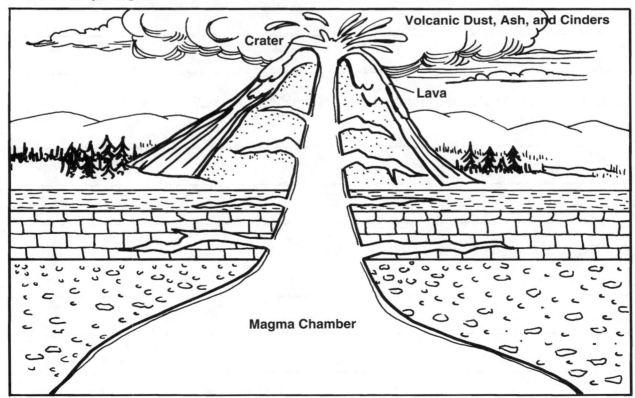

Diagram of an erupting volcano

Name _____   Date _____

For the student:

1. What is the difference between magma and lava?

_____

_____

_____

2. What is a volcanic crater?

_____

_____

_____

3. What is the vent?

_____

_____

_____

4. Why does light-colored magma cause volcanic explosions?

_____

_____

_____

5. What are volcanic bombs?

_____

_____

_____

Cinders and Shields
Types of Volcanoes

There are three basic types of volcanoes. They form in different ways. Let's take a look at the three.

Cinder Cone	Shield	Composite Cone
Cinders and rock particles are blown into the air.	Lava quietly flows from the vent.	A violent eruption sends up volcanic bombs, cinders and ash. A quiet volcanic flow follows the explosion. Alternating layers continue forming the mountain.
The mountain is small.	The mountain covers a large area.	The mountain is large.
The mountain has steep sides.	The sides are gently sloped.	The sides are steep.
	The mountain is dome-shaped.	The mountain is cone-shaped.
Example: Paricutin, Mexico	Example: Mauna Loa, Hawaii	Examples: Mt. Vesuvius, Italy Mt. St. Helen's, Washington
	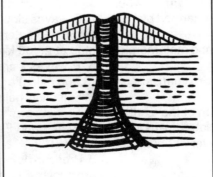	

Geology

ANSWER KEY

Earth: An Introduction (page 2)
1. We live in a spiral galaxy.
2. Our sun is medium-sized.
3. Temperatures would be too hot and radiation would be too strong for life to survive.
4. Temperatures would be too cold for life to survive.
5. Astronauts and cosmonauts have taken pictures during space flights.

The Formation of/The Structure of Earth (page 5)
1. Scientists do not know because they have not found conclusive evidence.
2. Scientists collect information by studying Earth, the Moon, and stars. Then they analyze the data and develop their theories.
3. If they know how a planet formed, they may be able to determine what will happen in the future.
4. Heavy metals are denser than other materials, so they are pulled down farther by gravity.
5. The crust is the outermost layer.
6. Direct observation is the gathering of information using your senses: sight, taste, feel, smell, hearing.
7. Scientists cannot study the inside of the Earth using direct observation.
8. Scientists have drilled into the Earth and have used seismographic equipment to collect data.
9. A model is a representation of something that cannot be studied easily or directly.
10. The Earth's layers are: inner core, outer core, mantle, crust.

Thin Crust or Thick Crust Diagram (page 7)
A. ocean; B. mountain; C. sial layer; D. sima layer

The Earth's Crust/Thin Crust or Thick Crust? (page 8)
1. Sedimentary rock is formed when Earth materials are worn away, then deposited in layers. Igneous rock is formed when magma cools deep within Earth or near its surface. Metamorphic rock is formed when sedimentary and igneous rocks are changed by heat and pressure.
2. The bedrock is a layer of igneous and metamorphic rock beneath sedimentary rock.
3. The most abundant elements are: oxygen, silicon, aluminum, iron, calcium.
4. The lithosphere is the solid portion of the Earth.
5. Scientists believe Earth's crustal plates are moving.
6. The ocean crust is the sima, a layer of basalt-like rock found beneath the oceans.
7. The two layers are the sial and the sima.
8. The sima continues under the oceans.
9. The sima's rocks are denser than those of the sial.

Elements in the Crust (page 9)
The symbols are: Oxygen (O), Silicon (Si), Aluminum (Al), Iron (Fe), Calcium (Ca), Sodium (Na), Potassium (K), and Magnesium (Mg).
1. Oxygen is the most common element in the crust.
2. Oxygen and silicon make up 83.8% of the crust's atoms.
3. Oxygen is a gas.
4. A gas will expand to fill a greater volume than a liquid.
5. Silicon would be most abundant because oxygen would not be found in the actual rocks and minerals.

The Mantle/The Core (page 13)
1. The Moho is like the membrane between the shell and white of an egg.
2. The mantle is like the white of an egg.
3. The mantle may become denser because there is more iron deeper into the mantle.
4. Temperatures become hotter deeper into the mantle.
5. The rocks are hot enough to melt; however, pressure prevents complete melting so the rocks achieve a state of plasticity.
6. The core is 3,550 kilometers (2,206 miles) deep.
7. The inner core is solid; the outer core is liquid.
8. The inner core has great pressure keeping it solid.
9. The Earth's core contains dense iron, which creates an effect similar to the magnetic field surrounding a magnet.
10. There is a lot more matter pressing down on the inner core than there is on the surface.

How Do You Find the Core?/Some Like it Hot (page 16)
1. The core is too far, and scientists do not have the technology to drill that far.
2. Seismic waves are shock waves created by earthquakes.
3. P-waves travel slowly through liquids. S-waves stop; they do not travel through liquids at all.
4. P-waves slow down at depths of 2,900 kilometers–5,150 kilometers (1,800–3,200 miles) and S-waves stop at 2,900 kilometers (1,800 miles).
5. P-waves increase their speed at 5,150 kilometers (3,200 miles) again.
6. Scientists believe the inner core is 5,000° C (9,032° F).
7. Space and Earth's atmosphere may have cooled its crust.
8. Pressure is less near the surface and temperatures are cooler. Pressure increases deeper into Earth, as do temperatures.

58

Geology

ANSWER KEY

9. If all radioactive material were to complete its decomposition, heat would no longer be released, and Earth might go through a cooling process.

10. Scientists cannot make direct observations or collect absolute evidence to prove their theories.

The Continental Drift Theory (page 18)

1. Wegener noticed the shapes of the continents and believed they could have fit together.
2. Wegener didn't have enough evidence to prove his theory.
3. It was about 45 years before new evidence was uncovered, supporting Wegener's theory.
4. The evidence indicated Africa, Australia, and India were once connected because the seeds were too large for wind to carry them very far.
5. The evidence indicated that South America, Africa, and Antarctica were once connected because the animal couldn't swim great distances.

From Pangaea to North America (page 19)

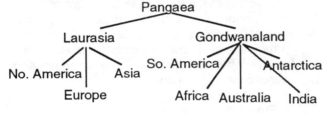

Ocean Floor Spreading/Plate Tectonics Theory (page 21)

1. Prior to the 1950s, scientists didn't have the equipment or technology to study the ocean floor.
2. They discovered underwater ridges and mountains.
3. Mid-ocean ridges are underwater mountains.
4. New rocks form along the ridges and push older rock away from the ridge.
5. Crust is pushed down toward the mantle and melts, replenishing the magma supply.
6. The lithosphere is the solid part of Earth: the crust and upper mantle.
7. The asthenosphere is the hot, fluid portion of the mantle.
8. The lithosphere has seven major plates.
9. The Pacific plate is the largest and the only plate that does not contain both continental and ocean crust.
10. Convection currents within the mantle move the plates.

Which Way Do You Go? (page 22)

A. Fracture (fault)
B. Convergent (type 2)
C. Spreading
D. Convergent (type 1)

Plate Movement: In, Out, and Sideways (page 23)

1. Plate boundaries are places where lithospheric plates meet.
2. At a spreading zone, two plates move apart and new crust is usually formed.
3. Earthquakes may occur at a fault zone.
4. Volcanoes may form at converging zones when one plate slides over another.
5. Folded mountains may be created when plates meet head-on at converging zones.
6. a. Fracture (fault); b. Convergent (type 2); c. Spreading; d. Convergent (type 1)

Surface Activity on Earth (page 25)

1. The processes that changed the Earth in the past are still in existence today.
2. Weathering is the breaking down of the lithosphere by agents of change.
3. The lithosphere is the solid part of Earth: the crust and upper mantle.
4. No, weathering never stops because substances are always exposed to the atmosphere.
5. Everything exposed to the atmosphere is affected by weathering.

Mechanical Weathering/Chemical Weathering (page 28)

1. Mechanical weathering is the process of breaking rock into smaller pieces.
2. The peeling or flaking of rocks parallel to the rock's surface due to repeated change from hot to cold is exfoliation.
3. Repeated freezing and thawing of water in cracks or holes is ice wedging.
4. Root-pry is the breaking of rock by expanding roots.
5. Landslides, caused by gravity, cause rocks to collide with each other and break.
6. Mechanical weathering changes only the size of the rock, while chemical weathering changes its composition, too.
7. Oxidation, a type of chemical weathering, produces rust.
8. When carbon dioxide combines with rain water, acid rain forms.
9. Acid rain is an example of carbonation.
10. Humic acids are acids produced by plants.

How Fast Does Weathering Occur? (page 30)
1. Sandstone weathers easily and granite is resistant.
2. Rocks that have cracks or holes that allow water to gather will be susceptible to oxidation and carbonation, etc.
3. A tropical climate, hot and wet, is most conducive to weathering.
4. When more fossil fuels are burned it creates more carbon dioxide in the air, which forms more acid rain, which weathers rocks.
5. Deserts have little moisture and less drastic temperature changes throughout the year.

Weathering: A Graphic Organizer (page 31)

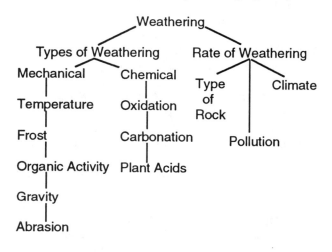

Weathering Experiments (page 32–33)
Experiment #1:
1. The ice line should be higher.
   Water expands as it freezes.
2. Water expands in rocks, causing mechanical weathering.
Experiment #2:
1. The marble should crack.
2. Temperature change causes cracking and exfoliation.
Experiment #3:
1. They change color, becoming darker as they become wet.
2. Sand should dry out and return to normal color. Steel wool should rust.
3. Oxidation and evaporation caused the changes.
4. Precipitation would have a similar effect on iron.

Erosion and Deposition (page 35)
1. Weathering is the breaking down of the lithosphere by agents of change. Erosion is the process of carrying away weathered material. Deposition is the process of laying down weathered material in a new location.
2. Wind, water, ice, waves are agents of erosion.
3. The Grand Canyon took 3 million years to form as it is now.
4. Flood waters damaging levees occurs rapidly.
5. Floods may destroy crops and homes.

Agent H₂0: Water
Assignment: Runoff/Assignment: Rivers (page 38)
1. Precipitation is water returning to Earth.
2. It becomes runoff.
3. Warm climates reduce runoff because evaporation increases, and cold climates reduce runoff because precipitation is trapped.
4. Steep slopes increase speed and amount of runoff. Flat areas have the opposite effect.
5. Answers will vary.
6. Gravity pulls mountain runoff downhill.
7. Sediment is weathered material.
8. The speed of a river and the amount of water it holds determine the amount of sediment it can carry.
9. The suspended load is small particles of sediment, while the bed load is large particles.
10. An immature river runs through a V-shaped valley, has fast moving water, has rapids and waterfalls, and experiences lots of erosion.

Agent Freezeout: Glaciers
Assignment: Poles and Mountains/Assignment: Destroy and Create (page 42)
1. A glacier is a large mass of moving ice and snow, which serves as an agent of change.
2. Alpine glaciers are found in old river valleys high in the mountains.
3. An ice cap is a continental glacier.
4. Gravity and the weight of the ice cause valley glaciers to move.
6. A glacier that is melting faster than it is moving is a retreating glacier.
7. A terminal moraine forms at the front edge of a glacier, and a lateral moraine forms along its side.
8. Moraines help scientists learn where glaciers formed and how far they moved.
9. Till is glacial drift that is not sorted by water; outwash is drift that is sorted by water.
10. Kettle lakes are formed when blocks of glacial ice are covered by debris and then melt slowly.

ANSWER KEY

Agent Splishsplash: Waves
Assignment: From Sea to Shining Sea/
Assignment: Beaches, Bars, and Spits (page 45)
1. A wave is a curling swell of water caused by wind, tides, or an earthquake.
2. The factors are wave size, wave force, weather, and the type of rock on the shore.
3. The waves break because they are slowing down and are affected by gravity.
4. The wave action enlarges the holes/cracks and can eventually break the rocks.
5. That is mechanical weathering.
6. Stacks, caves, and arches are formed by wave erosion.
7. Beaches are areas of deposition parallel to the shore.
8. Beaches of different kinds of rock may be different colors.
9. Beaches change because the water/waves continue to erode and deposit rocks.
10. A spit is a sandbar connected to the shore.

Agent Blowhard: Wind
Assignment: Deflation/Assignment: Tell Me How It's Dune (page 48)
1. Wind is moving air.
2. Wind is less damaging than water because it cannot hold as much material.
3. Wind is not dense enough to carry large particles up high.
4. The hard rocks protect the less resistant poles from wind damage.
5. Wind erosion is mechanical weathering.
6. A wind break slows the wind and reduces damage.
7. Trees, shrubs, and fences can be effective.
8. The slipface is the back side of a dune, away from the blowing wind.
9. Dunes move with the wind.
10. Loess is fertile soil created by wind erosion.

Subsurface Activity: Mountains (page 50)
1. Volcanic mountains are formed when magma is forced out of the crust.
2. Folded mountains are the most common.
3. Plate movement provides the force that moves the folded layers up.
4. The fault lines create steep-sided mountains.
5. Catskills: erosion
   Sierra Nevadas: fault block
   Mauna Loa: Volcano
   Rockies: folded
   Black Hills: dome

Mountains: Their Formation (page 51)
A. Eroded; Catskills
B. Folded: Alps, Rockies, etc.
C. Dome; Black Hills
D. Fault Block; Sierra Nevadas

The Moving Earth: Earthquakes (page 53)
1. They are primary (P-waves), secondary (S-waves), and surface (L-waves).
2. The focus is the place where an earthquake actually occurs.
3. The epicenter is the spot on the Earth's surface directly above the focus.
4. The Richter Scale measures the quake's magnitude.
5. Fires might start from broken gas lines or downed power lines.

Volcanoes: Mountains of Fire (page 56)
1. Magma is molten rock within the Earth, and lava is magma that has reached the surface.
2. A crater is a steep-sided hole at the top of a volcano.
3. The vent is the opening from which lava flows.
4. Light-colored magma hardens in the vent, building up pressure behind it.
5. Volcanic bombs are fragments of lava larger than 5 millimeters.

Bibliography

Bacon, Ernest and Richard Nastasi. *Earth-Space Sciences.* Austin: Steck-Vaughn Company, 1976.

Bishop, Margaret, et al. *Focus on Earth Science.* Westerville, Ohio: Charles E. Merrill Publishing Co., 1981.

Coble, Charles R., et al. *Earth Science.* Englewood Cliffs, New Jersey: Prentice Hall, Inc., 1984.

Current Science. 1992–1993 editions. Middletown, Connecticut: Weekly Reader Corporation.

Hackett, Dr. Jay K., et al. *Science.* Westerville, Ohio: Merrill Publishing Company, 1989.

Rosen, Seymour. *Earth Science Workshop 1.* New York: Globe Book Company, 1977.

Understanding Science and Nature: Planet Earth. Alexandria, Virginia: Time–Life Books, Inc., 1992.